DAVE BIDINI

FOR THOSE ABOUT TO WRITE

HOW I LEARNED TO LOVE BOOKS AND WHY I HAD TO WRITE THEM

TUNDRA BOOKS

Published in Canada by Tundra Books,
75 Sherbourne Street, Toronto, Ontario M5A 2P9

Published in the United States by Tundra Books of Northern New York,
P.O. Box 1030, Plattsburgh, New York 12901

Library of Congress Control Number: 2007920589

Library and Archives Canada Cataloguing in Publication

Bidini, Dave
    For those about to write : how I learned to love books and why I had to write
them / Dave Bidini.

ISBN 978-0-88776-769-2

    1. Authorship – Vocational guidance – Juvenile literature.
2. Bidini, Dave – Authorship – Juvenile literature.   I. Title.

PN153.B43 2007   j808'.02023   C2007-900220-X

We acknowledge the financial support of the Government of Canada through the
Book Publishing Industry Development Program (BPIDP) and that of the
Government of Ontario through the Ontario Media Development Corporation's
Ontario Book Initiative. We further acknowledge the support of the Canada
Council for the Arts and the Ontario Arts Council for our publishing program.

The excerpt on pages 45–46 is from *The Knife in My Hands* by Keith Maillard,
revised edition published as *Running* by Brindle & Glass Publishing. Copyright
© 2005 by Keith Maillard. Used by permission of Brindle & Glass Publishing.

Design: Scott Richardson

Printed and bound in Canada

1 2 3 4 5 6   12 11 10 09 08 07

For Dinah,
who got me this far

CONTENTS

INTRODUCTION

Hello, young writer, and good-bye. I know you won't be sticking around, and that's fine by me. You see, I've suffered the same problem all my life. I get so excited and inspired whenever I read good writing that I put down whatever's in my hands and rush to my sketchbook, where I peck and stab and scratch and scribble until I'm back writing in that beautiful, lonely little cocoon of life. While this certainly isn't the rule with every book, I'm the master of the quarter-finished read, the duke of the distracted. I'm the guy who, when asked whether he liked a certain book, almost always responds, "Well, the beginning was tremendous!" If I finish a book, it probably means that I didn't like it and that the beginning wasn't tremendous. In fact, I'm sure I would have stopped reading this book a few sentences ago were I not charged with the responsibility of writing it.

Jay Leno, the comedian and television host, once said that whenever he runs comedy workshops for young performers, the best pupils always leave after the first half. These students can't stand talking about comedy when what they really need, want, or have to do is perform or write comedy. Nothing makes a writer better than the act of writing, not even reading a text as fabulous, wise, and noble – if mildly untremendous – as this one. Really, if I achieve anything with this book, I'll have kept you from stuffing it hard and fast into the garburator, prompting you to wait until at least page sixty-six, when things really heat up, exploding into a thousand indispensable truths about the writer's essential role in the universe.

Writers write in a bubble of their own dreamy unconsciousness, but the act of writing can be terribly reactive. My first literary achievement as a teenager came as the result of my disdain for an English teacher, Mr. Romkema. Mr. Romkema made us read boring books (they had to be boring; I finished every one of them), and, worse, he talked about them ad nauseam in a voice that had all the intensity of an elevator's hum. He made long, boring books seem longer and more boring. So, when he announced that he was assigning a project that required every student to write a short story, I spent the next few evenings holed up in my room composing a small tale about a group of suspicious characters hanging out in a diner in the 1950s. There was no story; it was just a bunch of scenes strung together that I hoped would annoy Mr. Romkema.

I handed in the story, and then, a few classes later, Mr. Romkema announced that he wanted to see me after class. Satisfied that I'd upset him to the point where what he needed to say to me couldn't be said in public, I listened with self-righteous indignation until he told me, "David, your story was excellent. You have real talent as a writer. I would have published it in the yearbook were it not past the deadline."

I felt both horrible and wonderful at the same time, which is a sensation that pretty much sums up what it feels like to be a writer anyway. I'd be hiding from the truth if I didn't tell you that the act of writing books is a prolonged episode of stress, anxiety, and self-doubt punctuated with tiny moments of joy. It's hard to explain this to anyone who hasn't written before because, for the most part, whenever non-writers watch writers write, we come across as either lazy, half-asleep, entranced, insane, or near-dead.

Admittedly, writing doesn't look like much. One of the reasons why most of the kids in your class would rather be anything other than a writer is because the physical act of writing reveals only the inactivity, frustration, and madness of the craft, never the supreme emotional payoff. The life of an auto mechanic, say, must seem wildly thrilling compared to the life of a writer. The mechanic gets to wield heavy instruments and control great machines, while the writer gets to sit around – or, if you're American literary legend Ernest Hemingway, stand around – sweating over a piece of paper, usually at a small table with the drapes drawn and the sound of the tap dripping.

Very few young people think, "Man, a writer's life seems so thrilling," especially in a culture – particularly in North America – where billionaire rappers and svelte athletes and glamorous actors set the standard for wizardry on earth. Even lawyers – who also spend hours sweating over pieces of paper – have a better reputation in popular culture, played, at least on the silver screen, by big-name actors such as Al Pacino and Paul Newman.

By contrast, two recent films about writers dealt with the slow madness of Iris Murdoch and the self-destructive obsessions of Truman Capote, respectively. Murdoch was played with quiet and glorious vérité by Dame Judy Dench and Capote by Philip

Seymour Hoffman, though neither actor got to fire Tasers, hang around with Vin Diesel, or drive cars with gold-plated hubcaps. As a result, I'm guessing that very few of your friends are walking around wearing baseball caps with IRIS stitched in chains on the front. You could argue that the poets Lord Byron and Dylan Thomas lived wicked and fabulous lives, but because neither of them ever drove a flame-throwing Hummer or partied with Beenie Man, the idolatry of their work is limited to small handfuls of people smart enough to know that art is about getting it done as opposed to how you look doing it.

I love writers and writing because appearance has nothing to do with anything. (Though, alarmingly, personal image in publishing is gaining increasing importance.) For instance, as I carve out this very sentence, I look pale and bloated. There's food on my chin and I haven't bathed in ten days. But really, that I'm dressed in a torn-collared T-shirt and mustard-stained jeans has very little to do with what I'm typing on my keyboard. Until just now, you probably had no idea what the guy who wrote these sentences looked like, nor did you care.

I threw around a lot of ideas for this book. (Ah, lesson number one: always play around with words and ideas until you're happy with what's on the page.

American novelist Joseph Heller, who wrote *Catch-22*, had composed an entire novel before he realized the story would be better told by a minor character who, up to that point, had lurked in the background of the narrative. He rewrote the entire book from this perspective, adding several years to the writing process.) Essentially, the book that you're now holding jumps around a little, but I've tried to touch on as many creative issues and publishing tips as possible, pausing on the way to relate some interesting and insightful stories about writers and their lives. The form of this book – though not the rhythm – is a little higgledy-piggledy, but that's also the nature of composition and writing. Sometimes when you start scribbling, you have no idea where you'll end up (unless you're Russo-American novelist Vladimir Nabokov, who carefully charted out his sentences on index cards), but that's part of the thrill too: watching that curiously colored snake unfurl from your mind to your hand to the page. Really, it's all about starting, because if you can't start, you can't end. You'll leave only ravaged fingernails and half-drained coffee cups bubbling with mold, and no life-affirming somersaults through the bountiful garden of God and art.

So, hey, let's start.

PAPER AND CARDBOARD

Books is good. They smell good – mashed tree bits
stamped with ink and machine grease – and even
those found in the back of thrift stores under piles of
old shoes and underwear are not entirely objection-
able. Books look good too: their clean black-on-
white print, their enchanting cover art, their thin
spines that peek out like sentries from the shelves.
Books even sound good. They're quiet, still, and
bother no one, which, in our modern era of sonic
madness and electronic rabble, provides an elegant
respite from so much annoying media.

Apart from my childhood's spit-soaked, well-
teethed toys, books were among my first possessions
(my mother wrote my name on the inside of the front
covers to prove my ownership of them). They were
also the first important things entrusted to me in a
world where DON'T TOUCH was ascribed to pretty
much all other adult items in the house. My and my

sister's bookcases – filled with C.S. Lewis, Dr. Seuss, Edgar Rice Burroughs, Ogden Nash – were no one's but our own, wooden fortresses of words that concealed deep, secret thoughts. A lot of things represent the creative mind of a child, but a bookcase spilling with half-chewed, dog-eared, bow-spined books reveals a young person's tempest of thought.

Growing up, books were precious yet commonplace, sacred yet playful. Even though my treasured *Land of the Dinosaurs* and *Mammals of the World* series were in good condition, I knew that no matter how many times they fell from my school bag and became swallowed by mud that the knowledge I'd gleaned from their contents remained. Because my parents had read these books to me on demand ad nauseam, their words existed long after in my thoughts. Growing up, books were almost parental in their own right, passing on knowledge and information before leaving me to transfer that knowledge into power.

When I was a kid, writing seemed like something that anyone could do, like playing hopscotch or throwing a ball. At school and at home, someone was always putting a crayon, marker, pencil, pencil crayon, or piece of chalk in my hand and trying to get me to write or draw or scribble whatever came to mind. I liked the weight of the instrument in my hand, gripped, at first, like a blunt bone in my fist, and then, once I learned how, pinched between a pyramid of fingers, the eraser or end or pen lid slivering up from my grip, and the point of the instrument stabbing or poking or scratching or tickling the flat of whatever surface had become my canvas of the moment.

I was writing books before I even called them that, stapling torn-up pictures and nonsense scribbles between two sheets of paper and then writing a few words in color on the cover. In a slow and quiet way, I was being prepared for my literary adulthood, because the process of creating books is, more or less, the same at six as it is at sixty, only with better grammar. Whenever I'm marking up a blank page or screen, my mind follows the same rabbit of imagination down the same deep hole of thought, at which point I become free from the boundaries of clock time to travel through passageways of creativity that always feel new and strange and wild, even though I've visited them millions of times before.

MY FIRST BOOK

I remember the exact moment when I knew that I wanted to write books or, rather, that I *could* write books. It happened in Grade 7 history class. We were asked to write an assignment based on a historical figure, and I chose Jacques Cartier. I tried creating a mock journal – or travel log – that Cartier himself might have written while traveling throughout Canada in the 1500s. I used a hard-bound journal – I think my mother had bought it for me at the local drugstore in Etobicoke's Westway Plaza – and burnished the pages with a matchstick to give them an old, weathered look, as if they'd been singed by candlelight while Cartier scribbled away in his cabin at night. The project yielded the best mark I'd ever got in a class – A – but it wasn't so much the singularity of the work or the praise from my teacher that pleased me; it was the notion that I'd created something that looked, felt, and read like a real book.

MOM/DAD

The prospect of having to choose a direction in life can be daunting, especially when young writers find themselves drawn along a pathway of art rather than commerce. It doesn't help that very few parents pop champagne corks and rejoice in the streets after learning that their son or daughter is planning a "career in letters." Most treat the news as they would the announcement of a debilitating illness or prison sentence. A writer's life ensures a difficult financial situation as well as emotional instability. Even someone such as J.K. Rowling, author of the Harry Potter series, wrote her first book in cafés while unemployed and struggling as a single mother.

Still, no matter how resistant Mom/Dad might be to the young writer's dream, we can all be grateful that we aren't Jeanette Winterson. This acclaimed British novelist had deeply religious parents who forbade her from reading or writing literature, even though she was encouraged to compose sermons, which she was doing by the time she was eight. Young Jeanette was forced to hide books under her clothes and do most of her reading behind a locked bathroom door (her parents only owned six books, two of them Bibles). She took to stashing books under her mattress – she'd hidden seventy-seven of them – and the plan worked quite well until her mother noticed that Jeanette's bed was slowly rising, at which point her mother tore the mattress apart and burned everything. This early demonization of literature probably fed Jeanette's sense of adolescent rebellion and resulted in a successful, well-regarded career.

THE GOOD DOCTOR

A lot of my first storybooks were written by Theodor Geisel, aka Dr. Seuss. Reading Dr. Seuss is a universal literary experience because his books have been translated throughout most of the world. *Green Eggs and Ham* and *How the Grinch Stole Christmas* – with their playful, simple "Seussist" language – made it seem as if anyone could write books, and that you didn't have to use big, important-sounding words. Seuss's unique style came about in 1960 when a friend challenged him to write a book using no more than fifty words. This challenge resulted in the strange and beloved *Cat in the Hat*, which, because of its simple vocabulary and rare energy, went on to sell millions of copies and produce a kazillion more writers.

THE BIDINIS

I was lucky that my parents were encouraging when it came to my artistic tendencies. They probably had a lot of time to get used to it, because I took to scribbling at an early age. I'd spend hours sitting at my father's desk in our basement, hammering out nonsense on an old Underwood typewriter – the same kind of machine upon which J.K. Rowling wrote *Harry Potter and the Philosopher's Stone* – with the energy that other kids might have brought to their toy trucks or Lego. I loved the sound of the keys in flight as they sprung from the typewriter's chassis and *shhuunked* upon striking the paper; the way my fingertips felt on the shiny, worn faces of the keyboard; and the scent of the ribbon's ink as it mixed with the typewriter grease and the warm smell of whatever was cooking in the kitchen upstairs. Because old typewriters were iron-heavy and impossible for me to lift, I felt like I was lording over a great machine or, better yet, taming it with my tiny hands. Unlike other household appliances – things you simply turned on with a button – the typewriter was a contraption that sat broodingly on the desk until the music of my fingers brought it to life.

Working on the typewriter also meant that people left me alone to write. The time I spent sitting in the curtained light of the basement was mine and no one else's, and those sessions at the keyboard got me used to spending hours in my own head. After a while, I understood the interior experience as positive and productive. As a writer and a person, I never felt socially withdrawn, even though writing meant I would retreat from the rest of the world. I considered the solitude and thoughtfulness of writing to be a strength rather than a weakness. I also knew that, despite the heroic nature of characters such as Tarzan, Batman, Sinbad, or the Three Musketeers, they'd likely been invented by a shy person sitting in a room alone bent over a keyboard, and that few bullies would have ever thought themselves tough or cool had movie villains or adventure-book scoundrels not been written by the very nerds upon whom they preyed. In fact, Tarzan's creator, Edgar Rice Burroughs, was no more than a simple pencil-sharpener salesman when he invented his jungle hero.

SUPERWORDS

When they weren't dueling villains hell-bent on destroying the world, both Superman and Spider-Man had newspaper jobs. They made the world of journalism seem exciting, even compared with what they did the rest of the time. Clark Kent, aka Superman, worked as a mild-mannered reporter for the *Daily Planet* newspaper, whose newsroom was familiar to any comic book–reading kid. There were lots of exciting moments where the buzz of a break-ing story – SUPERMAN SUFFERS KRYPTONITE BLAST!; SUPERMAN DISARMS RADIOACTIVE ROCKET HEADING FOR EARTH! – set the newsroom alight, making it seem like an enthralling and sus-penseful place to work.

Peter Parker, Spider-Man's alter ego, was a news-paper photographer when he wasn't swinging high above greater Manhattan. The environment at Parker's paper – the *Daily Bugle* – was more hostile

than the *Daily Planet*'s, ruled over, as it was, by
J. Jonah Jameson, a cantankerous, cigar-chomping
tyrant who introduced in me a great and unreasonable fear and suspicion of all editors. Still, Parker's
workplace teemed with sound and life, making it
seem as if the newspaper had been a perfect breeding
ground for Spider-Man's high-wire adventures.

EDDIE

As a pre-teen, I wrote television reviews, stories, and poems. My parents suggested that I submit one of my poems – about Eddie Shack, the colorful Toronto Maple Leafs hockey player of the late 1960s and early 1970s – to a local newspaper, the *Toronto Sun*. When I was growing up – and certainly now, in 2007 – there were three newspapers with weekend kids' sections featuring the work of teenagers and pre-teens. Today's young writers should contact the people who run these sections in an attempt to get published. Folks who work with teenage **prose** (any kind of writing that's not in verse form) tend to be sympathetic and encouraging (at least they were to me) and, as you'll see on the next page, none too picky when it comes to what they will or won't publish.

At the risk of ruining my esteemed literary reputation – and in the name of artistic humility – here is my poem reprinted from the *Toronto Sun*:

MY IDOL

When he's on the ice
He always tries
But carrying the puck
He really flies
Playing the man
And shooting hard
When on defence
He's like a guard
Flashing skates
And scoring goals
Like a bowling ball
He always rolls
Off the ice
He's Eddie Shack
So when you meet him
Clear the track

As you can see, my early work was nothing like the work of author Paul Bowles, who wrote and illustrated a novel when he was four, or *The Jungle Book*'s Rudyard Kipling, who was a literary star at twenty-four, or the young British writer William Dalrymple, whose acclaimed travel book, *Xanadu*, was published when he was twenty-two. Still, being published at eleven in the *Toronto Sun* helped me realize three things: one, being published meant getting rewarded with a cool "Young Sun" T-shirt; two, the professional writing game didn't appear to be nearly as difficult to crack as, say, the world of doctoring, space travel, professional hockey, daredeviling, or nuclear physics; and three, sending out one's work didn't necessarily mean being laughed at or ridiculed or driven into a deeper corner of the basement, as I had feared. Had I been rebuffed by the *Toronto Sun*, I don't know how I would have responded, but I'm pretty sure my parents would have kept sending out my hockey verse until somebody saw the light, using their gentle hand to raise me onto a pedestal of confidence from which I would stand and holler at the world.

WRITERS ON TV

There's a feeling in certain corners of the literary community that part of television's agenda is to steer the public's attention away from books. And while it's true that watching television generally requires less attention or brainwork than reading books, it was the idiot box that first made me aware of writers and their lives.

In the 1970s, Oscar Madison was one-half of *The Odd Couple*, a TV sitcom based on the play of the same name. Madison was played by Jack Klugman. His roommate was Felix Unger, played by Tony Randall. While the two divorced men had an adversarial relationship, they were bound together, adrift in the big city.

Oscar Madison was a sportswriter. Many of the show's episodes focused on his troubles in the press boxes and dressing rooms of local New York teams; through these vignettes, I understood that actual writers were responsible for the stories I read in the newspaper every morning.

I began studying the names of Toronto's sports columnists – real-life Oscar Madisons such as Jim Vipond, Jim Hunt, Dick Beddoes, Trent Frayne, and Milt Dunnell – until I became familiar with their colorful styles and techniques. After a while, I wrote them letters. They wrote back words of encouragement – work hard, listen to your parents, write as often as possible – on paper stained with coffee-cup rings and cigar ashes. One letter, from the late *Toronto Sun* columnist Jim "Shaky" Hunt, was awkwardly written with poor spelling, which proved that you didn't have to be a grammatical genius to write for the newspaper. This made it much easier to imagine myself working for one. Over the years, I've written lots of letters to writers and musicians. Not to generalize about the rock-and-roll community, but no musician has ever written me back. Writers, however, have always answered the call.

The first few times I visited a **press box** – the section of an arena high above the rink or playing field where people who work for the media observe sports or entertainment events – I found myself among these very writers. After attending a press conference for an international hockey tournament,

I noticed Jim Hunt getting on an escalator in the
Sheraton Hotel. He was rumpled and slow-footed,
with a broad, cartoonish face. I wanted to tell him
how much his letter had meant to me, how apprecia-
tive I was that he'd written back, so I approached
him from behind. This proved to be the wrong tact,
however, for I startled him badly. He jumped back as
if I'd drawn a switchblade on him, listened to me
with great suspicion, and then peeled away as soon
as the escalator reached the top.

There also used to be a popular television show
in the 1970s called *The Waltons*. It took place in
wartime during the 1940s and featured a farm family
struggling to stay out of poverty. One of the main
characters was the Waltons' oldest son, John Boy,
who wanted to be a writer.

John Boy (played by Richard E. Thomas) was a
good guy who was always trying to do the right
thing. Being a virtuous, careful kid myself, I related
to John Boy, and because he wanted to be a writer, I
wanted to be one too. This was actually the first time
I realized that someone could actually be a writer, as
opposed to someone who just wrote. Even though
John Boy struggled, he ended up getting pieces published (which made me aware of publishers) that
paid little or no money (which made me wary of

publishers). Still, there was something memorable about the way John Boy's pencil sounded scratching against the yellow tablet – the word *tablet* made it seem as if to write was to engrave scripture – and how a lot of the townsfolk rolled their eyes whenever John Boy announced his desire to write fiction. During the Walton years, I asked for, and received, yellow tablets from my parents. I remember laying them out on the kitchen table and arching over the paper, scratching it with my own pointed Hilroy, listening as much as thinking, filling page after page.

ALAN MAKI

Alan Maki used to be a writer for the *Etobicoke Gazette*, the community newspaper we received when I was growing up. At my parents' insistence, I sent him a letter requesting guidance and writing advice. One day, a small package stamped with the newspaper's logo arrived at our door, containing a note from Maki and his very own copy of the Strunk and White grammar guide, *The Elements of Style*. I'd never heard of it before, but I've since learned that it's one of the most well-regarded grammar handbooks ever published and one of the easiest to understand. Whenever a writer needs to find, out, where, or where not, to place a comma, or whether to use *italics* to *stress* a thought, or how to deploy – or not deploy – a two-dash break, Strunk and White can help.

Maki's note said that the book had seen him through his literary upbringing, and that he hoped it would do the same for me. Years later, he went on to become a well-respected and much-loved *Globe and Mail* sportswriter, and I had the opportunity to meet him in Calgary in 1994. I told him the story of the handbook he'd sent me, but he'd forgotten all about it. Still, when I said that his gesture had made it seem to me as if all scribes were good and honorable people, his eyes misted over with the realization that he'd helped a young writer, and that he'd done a good and proper thing.

THE *SUNSHINE NEWS*

Every scribbler has to start somewhere. For me, it was the *Sunshine News*, a national high-school music newspaper. The paper was as unlike *The New York Times* as I was unlike Hunter S. Thompson, who was an eccentric magazine reporter famous for sleeping next to a loaded rifle. The newspaper was full of delightful little tips such as where to buy a good backpack and interviews with teen heartthrobs of the day. Hundreds of thousands of copies were distributed monthly to schools, and I wanted badly to be in its pages.

The *Sunshine News*'s publishing empire consisted of a few modest offices on the bottom floor of a downtown Toronto building. In subsequent years, I've had the chance to walk the great press floors of Canada, but there was something about being in the *Sunshine News* building for the first time that remains my most vivid impression of life in the publishing world. It was like entering a rarified space filled with people who, remarkably, earned their living by putting out a newspaper. Had I been a kid obsessed with air travel, it would have been like climbing into the cockpit of a jet plane for the first time. I can still remember the chatter and whir of the office's electric typewriters; rotary telephones ringing one after another; staff members shuffling stories, ad copy, and art from one station to another; and, in the far corner of the room, the graphics/layout personnel clipping and gluing and squaring text and photographs to fill forty-plus pages of clumsy student prose.

During my first visit, I was greeted by the newspaper's publisher, a well-dressed German-Canadian fellow who seemed bemused by my strong desire to write for the paper. He introduced me to a young woman – the magazine's senior editor – who was friendly and important-looking.

At this point, I should probably explain what publishers and senior editors are, just in case you're about to proceed down this same journalistic path. A magazine or newspaper **publisher** is the person who oversees the operation – he or she hires most of the staff, creates a vision for the publication, and raises the money to get it going; sometimes the publisher even provides the money. The **senior editor** is the publisher's eyes and ears, working closely with the staff, and sometimes – but not always – editing the contributing writers' work. **Editing** is the process by which prose is altered so that it sort of reads as decent as it can kind of be as possible, which, were that last thought edited, would read: *altered to read as well as possible.* (For those of you who can't get enough about editing, there's more on this later in the book.)

When the senior editor asked about my interests, I told her that I wanted to write about movies, sports, and rock and roll. She pointed to a stack of records – they'd been sent, for free, to the paper for review purposes – told me to pick out whatever I liked, and suggested that I call her once they'd **put to bed** (sent to the printer) the latest edition of the paper.

My first assignment for the *Sunshine News* was to cover the World Music Festival, a day-long concert at Exhibition Stadium. I was asked to write a review of the show. For those who don't know, the idea behind a **review** is to pass on your impressions – usually in no more than five hundred to seven hundred words – of a concert, film, art exhibit, and so on. In the newspaper world, writers are employed as music, movie, art, television, book, and media **reviewers** – also known as **critics** – and their job is to report on the

.

circumstances of a certain event and whether, in the writer's opinion, the reader's time would be well spent attending the event. Writing reviews usually pays poorly – some reviews pay no more than $50 each, which, in 2007, is the same as what I was making with the *Sunshine News* – but for a young writer, it's a great way to sharpen your skills without having to tackle large-scale stories too early in your literary career.

For the World Music Festival, I brought along my best friend, Rick, who was hired to take photographs with his little automated camera. I remember being in the stadium on that sweltering July day with thirty thousand other fans and feeling that, because I was *reporting*, I somehow stood out from the crowd. The next day, I hauled our family's typewriter up to the kitchen table and wrote my review. Just completing the piece was, at that point, my single greatest literary achievement. And even though the article was only seven hundred words, it felt like an incredible length, considering that most of what I'd written before were little fifty-word tidbits.

I went on to write other concert and album reviews for the *Sunshine News*. Eventually, I acquired a **press pass** – a laminated card that gives the reviewer access to the press box and other comfortable sections with

a good view of the arena or theater, even backstage.
Things were going quite well in my junior reporter's
life until I was asked to review a Styx concert, after
which things got complicated.

I don't know if you know about Styx – I mean, you
probably shouldn't know about them; you should be
listening to bands such as Caribou, Spoon, and The
Books, instead – but Styx was a 1970s American
hard-rock/pop band whose big hit was "Come Sail
Away," from their monstrously popular album *The
Grand Illusion*. They were basically Queen lite, a
stadium rock band fronted by a Broadway singer.
The *Sunshine News* offered me tickets to their show
at Maple Leaf Gardens in Toronto, which also featured Prairie rockers Streetheart as the opening band.
I jumped at the chance.

Streetheart, it turned out, set the house on fire,
which made watching Styx even harder. While they
moved wildly around the stage and worked tirelessly
to win applause, Styx spent much of their show
hiding behind dry ice. They just stood there and
played their hits, drawing lazy cheers from the
crowd. I had no idea how to review their show
because it was the worst concert I'd ever seen. Up
until this point in my young journalist's life, I'd never
written bad things about a band before. In a way, I

wasn't even aware that reviewers were able to write negatively about what they'd seen because most articles in the *Sunshine News* were either overwhelmingly positive or neutral. Really, to criticize a band would have been to break from what seemed like editorial policy. The idea of writing about something I didn't like felt strange and unsettling.

I decided to write the truth. The headline of my story was STYX'S CHEAP ILLUSION. To its credit, the newspaper did nothing to sugarcoat the review. Days after the newspaper came out, angry Styx fans started calling my home. The calls came around the dinner hour, which annoyed my parents and humiliated me. Kids called me names, yelled, "You suck, man! You're dead! Styx rules!" It was horrible and I didn't know how to deal with it, but I quickly became aware of the power and influence of the written word. I learned the hard way that people took what they read seriously – even obnoxious teenage Styx fans – and that there was a price to pay for telling the truth, which proved to be a valuable life lesson. I finally got the courage to shout back at my assailants, empowered by the notion that, because I was a writer, I was also a guardian of truth. One evening, the voice on the other end of the line accused me: "You probably don't even like Max Webster [a progressive new-wave band]."

"Of course I like Max Webster. You probably don't even like AC/DC," I shot back.

"No way. I love AC/DC!" he said.

There was silence.

And then he hung up.

MAGS

Post-career, all writers want to be regarded as the great literary lions of their time, about whom lively and outrageous stories are rehashed in the worst bars and finest salons of the world. But a writer's life is also about the brass tacks: working when – and if – you want to, and earning enough money to get from one sheaf of words to the next.

Because getting published in the *Sunshine News* was, for me, like getting published in *The Washington Post*, I didn't grasp the realities of magazine writing until much later. Because the public spends more time thumbing through magazines than reading novels, magazine writing can translate into valuable exposure for young writers and important visibility (and readability) for established writers, whose work is sometimes difficult to grasp (or simply ignored) by the public at large. Magazine work also presents an ocean of opportunity, and if a writer wanted to devote their days to writing for a myriad of different magazines, they could. The twenty-first century has brought forth hundreds of specialty magazines, and while you wouldn't think that *Allergy Times* or *Skateboarders Anonymous* or *Yoga World* would sustain a devout readership, they're all potential employers for the motivated scribe.

Another positive to magazine writing is the money. Traditionally, successful mags – with their monthly stream of advertising revenue – pay writers well, and sometimes better than smaller publishing houses. In 2007 in Canada, a handful of magazines ascended to the dollar-per-word rate, and in some instances, I found myself earning more for long magazine pieces than for my short stories. Of course, books hang around on library shelves well after their publication date, while magazines last for as long as your coffee table stays messy and unsorted. Still, this difference is often ignored so that the writer can keep his or her feet moving and pay the rent.

Magazine writing would be a literary paradise were it not for the process of pitching ideas to get them assigned. **Pitching** means explaining what a proposed article will be like before you've actually written it. It's a challenge – and a bit of a rare skill – to explain what a story will be like before it exists.

Writers who are good – or, rather, experienced – at pitching are able to conjure the body and feel and narrative of an unwritten piece as if by magic. Their pitches – or **proposals** – are explained in few words and in a matter of minutes. Editors generally adhere to the maxim that if one has to struggle to explain what a story is – or will be about – it's probably not worth writing anyway.

It helps to be dogged and vigilant while pursuing story assignments in the wide world of mags. Like choosing book publishers, writers should turn to magazines *they* respect and admire. They should get to know the magazine's editorial feel and patterns of storytelling, then figure out how their own work might fit in. I'm not suggesting that you overthink this. I'm trying to be instructive here, but the ability to tell a good story is just as important as knowing what kind of story might best fit where. Still, appealing to like-minded editors is a way of getting your ideas heard by the right people and, ultimately, giving your voice the attention and life that it deserves.

Some Canadian magazines and newspapers also offer **internships**, when a person volunteers to work for a period of time in the office of a magazine, newspaper, or publishing company. These positions can be valuable to young writers trying to find their way. Of the last thirty-odd interns at *TORO* magazine, for instance, almost all have risen to greater literary heights. A friend of mine, who was one of *TORO*'s editors, told me that her interns have gone on to earn editorships at major magazines, the *National Post* newspaper, and *TORO* itself. Others have gone on to full-time freelance writing careers and even the prized journalism program at Columbia University in New York. In my friend's case, she said, "I started out as an intern at places that didn't even have interns, stuffing envelopes for free until it led to being offered my own **imprint** [a line of specific titles issued by a publishing company]. I copy edited a mag for free until it led to a real job at a newspaper, which I was offered after the editor saw the red-splattered **galleys** [a proof of typeset text] I'd marked up for the previous mag."

SCHOOLED

I discovered the *Sunshine News* in high school:
Kipling Collegiate Institute, Etobicoke, Ontario. The
best part of high school was Mr. Clark's English
class. There, I learned to use ink for something other
than scribbling band names on the legs of my Levi's.
Mr. Clark was an unusual sight, built like a large,
bespectacled goose with lenses as thick as silver
dollars. He spoke with a slight lisp and would occa-
sionally whirl light-footed about the room, quoting
the work of long-dead poets such as Keats or Shelley
to kids more familiar with TV sitcoms or comic
strips. (Mr. Clark was the anti–Mr. Romkema.) Every
now and then, he'd stand on a chair at the front of
the class and, possessing a booming voice, shout out
the critical section of whatever novel we were studying. Predictably, balls of crumpled paper snowed the
air, hitting Mr. Clark atop the head or in the chest,
knocking his glasses askew. Still, he was fearless in

the face of his numb-headed charges, roaring on with boundless literary enthusiasm. Through him, I was introduced to books by writers such as Ernest Hemingway and Franz Kafka, whose first names were as exotic to me as their last. The final week of the school year, I asked Mr. Clark if I could stand on the teacher's throne and read aloud from a book by James Joyce called *Portrait of the Artist as a Young Man*. Like Mr. Clark, I refused to be toppled.

It was in Mr. Clark's class that I crossed the bridge from reading adventure books, comics, and sports biographies to reading deeper, more resonant works. Not to disparage the general teaching community, but Mr. Clark's genius of communication and enthusiasm was rare, and during my high-school years, I spent lots of time on my own, trolling library shelves and picking out books that I'd never heard of before. Sometimes, I sought help from the librarians, but my relationship with them was as guarded and distant as it was with anybody twice my age.

I was certainly not the first young writer to seek literary refuge in a library. American author Gary Paulsen had a miserable, wandering childhood in which he followed his father's state-jumping career in the military. He was a chronically shy, sports-challenged young man whose life changed the moment he walked past the library in Thief River Falls, Minnesota, in the dead of winter. He went inside to get warm in the library's reading room, at which point the librarian asked if he needed a book to read. He did, and after ingesting a series of science-fiction, western, and classic titles, he became hooked on books. He eventually got a library card, which, Paulsen remembers, was "like being handed the world." This gave way to an interest in writing, but because he had no credentials, Paulsen invented some. Later on, he faked an impressive résumé – claiming he'd worked at a number of fine magazines and newspapers – and landed a job as an editor for a men's magazine. He was found out, but people at the magazine showed him the ropes until he started writing in earnest, eventually scribbling such heartfelt and beloved young-adult classics as *Woodsong* and *The Foxman*.

YES, IT AIN'T

Another source of literary guidance came from the
proprietors of a bookstore called This Ain't the
Rosedale Library in downtown Toronto. The shop
still exists today. Its original location was on Queen
Street East in a building that it shared with a record
store, The Record Peddler. The shop sat at the top of
a small staircase with a pinball machine on the
landing, the Peddler on the left, and the bookstore on
the right. It was paradise to a kid taken with books
and records. My parents would drop me off,
knowing that I'd spend the next four hours hanging
out listening to cool new records, reading sections of
great books, and feeding quarters into the pinball
machine. My friends and I would finish the afternoon staring at our purchases and grabbing a bite at
the Blue Sea diner across the street, where the burger/
fries/pop combo cost five dollars.

It was at the This Ain't the Rosedale Library bookstore where I met my first real writers: William S. Burroughs, Earle Birney, Lynda J. Barry, and countless others. What struck me most was how different they were from one another: Barry reminded me of a cool cousin you only saw once or twice every few years; Birney wore an oversized winter coat and carried newspapers rolled and stuffed under his arm; and Burroughs was dressed in a fine gray suit and dashing fedora. Unlike rock stars – who were all skinny, wild-haired, and tired-looking – and athletes – who had impossibly strong bodies and serious eyes – to be a writer, you could look however you wanted to look. You could be anybody and nobody.

THE KNIFE

The bookstore's two shopkeepers, Charlie and Dan,
introduced me to the literature of my early adulthood: *Bums* by Peter Golenblock, *King Leary* by
Paul Quarrington, Harvey Pekar's comics, the
Oberon Press editions of books by W.P. Kinsella, and
The Knife in My Hands by Keith Maillard. You
might not know who Keith Maillard is, but it doesn't
matter. Back in the early 1980s, no one knew him
either, but he still became my favorite writer. Keith
(or Mr. Maillard, which is probably what I'd call him
if I met him) isn't what anyone would consider a
giant of Canadian literature, at least not outside of
my household. Most adults, whose knowledge of
lawn-mowing and the driveway arts is probably
greater than their appreciation of contemporary
CanLit, know who Margaret Atwood and Mordecai
Richler are, but throw them a name such as Keith

Maillard and they'll likely harrumph and return to waving around their garden shears.

Still, despite his quiet literary status, Maillard's novels had a big impact on me. *The Knife in My Hands* is what reviewers might call a coming-of-age novel. During the years in which I "came of age" – fourteen to seventeen – this kind of book was pretty much all that I read. It focused on young people and the complications of their lives. It addressed issues that I couldn't discuss with my mom and dad – drugs, sexuality, violence, prejudice – another instance of books filling a quasi-parental role in my young reader's life.

The protagonist of Keith Maillard's first three novels – John Dupre – was, as I was, a young person searching for a world beyond his small town (for Dupre, it was Raysburg, West Virginia; for me, Etobicoke, Ontario). Through Dupre, I was able to emotionally relate to the prose. It was as if my life was being played out through the character's story. Smoking Camels in the front seat of my Delta 88 – or, rather, my parents' Delta 88 – parked against the edge of a frosted-over baseball diamond, was the first tactile reading experience I can remember: the weight of the hardcover, the chill of the season on my hands as I turned the pages, the upholstered cushions of the car supporting my back, the fat winter sun shining across the icy park, the pop of the cigarette lighter as it disengaged from the car's dashboard, and, of course, the hum of Maillard's easy prose buzzing across my thoughts. Whenever I'm asked to write about my formative literary experiences, I mention *The Knife in My Hands*, partly because it's a way of keeping the book's title alive, and partly because I can talk about it in a way that's personal.

Here is an excerpt:

> I was always attracted to extremes, willing to follow any promising line of thought as far as I could, no matter how strange the journey. But Lyle, when I first knew him (strangely enough, for all his insane Catholic fervor), would go only so far and then pull back.
>
> One afternoon at the tail end of winter, a sunny Saturday predicting spring, Lyle borrowed his father's car, picked me up, and we took off for a drive into the country. His father, a worried man, had made Lyle wait until he was seventeen to get his driver's license and then had told him plainly never to take the car out of town. So here we were, the first chance we got, headed out of town.

The car broke down just outside of Barnesville. We found a kid to help us fix it, one of those teenage automotive wizards who can repair anything with a set of open-end wrenches and a big hammer. While the kid was puttering around under the hood, I was playing the cool role, beginning every sentence with "man." Lyle stood by and wrung his hands.

After I acknowledged the book in a newspaper article a few years ago, Mr. Maillard's publisher contacted me on his behalf and asked if I'd write a comment for a new edition of the book. Having been recognized by one of my favorite authors – after spending the first part of my writing life scribbling countless bad imitations of his books in my own struggling attempt to become a writer – was the kind of reward I couldn't possibly have imagined. Selling tons of books and winning the occasional prize is nice, but being acknowledged by your hero is one of the foundations of artistic validation.

Besides *The Knife in My Hands*, I made other literary coming-of-age discoveries: *Be True to Your School* by Bob Greene, *Jack in the Box* by William Kotzwinkle, *The Apprenticeship of Duddy Kravitz* by Mordecai Richler, and *The Outsiders* and *Rumble Fish* by S.E. Hinton. A few of Hinton's teen-centric books were, in fact, written while she was coming-of-age. Her full name is Susan Eloise Hinton, but she used an abbreviated version so male readers wouldn't assume that because her books were written by a female, they were only meant for girls. Hinton started writing in her first year of high school as a way of coping with the death of her parents. She told stories about what she'd seen or experienced in her school in Tulsa, Oklahoma, reworking them into small, gripping novels about the lives of young people.

POSSIBLY THE KEY TO LITERARY
FAME AND ACHIEVEMENT

At the end of high school, I started working for *Shades* magazine, a smart, cool alternative Toronto pop tabloid. *Shades* paid about $100 a story, no matter the size. Writers got more or less the same dough, whether they were reviewing a local punk CD or writing three thousand words about illustrator and author Edward Gorey. Still, $100 to a kid with a substantial album- and book-buying habit was pretty great. If I squinted hard enough, I could almost see my first publishing **advance** (a payment made by a publisher to a writer prior to the completion or publication of a manuscript).

Shades kept its modest album reviews at the back of the magazine and filled its front pages with long, wordy essays and full-length black and white photographs. The layout was simple and prose-heavy. Today's Canadian magazines – such as *Maclean's* and *Toronto Life*, found in the waiting rooms of your doctor or dentist – are zippy, with small pieces that nibble the reader to death, at least at the beginning of the **book** (magazine people refer to their publication as a book because it gets **proofed** – combed by a set of eyes for printing, spelling, or grammatical errors – as a bound edition before going off to the printer). This kind of writing is justified – and defended – as a reflection of society's reduced attention span, but television and rock videos existed in the 1980s too, and that didn't stop *Shades* from hitting the reader with a long essay, accompanied by a beautiful portrait, on page four. It was closer in design and spirit to *The New Yorker* or *Harper's*, in which writers are given a sense of responsibility, knowing that their ideas won't be boxed into anecdotal **sidebars** (a brief addition to a main article) or shortened to make room for ad space (*Shades* relied on government grants and rarely turned a profit).

I've mentioned her in my other books, but it bears repeating that Sheila Wawanash was *Shades*'s editor. I probably wouldn't have set upon my literary course if she hadn't been so encouraging. Once, I sent her an unsolicited essay about my encounter with the new-wave band Devo – whose members wore plastic hair and performed on conveyor belts – despite having had it cruelly rejected by the editors of *New York*

Rocker magazine, who told me that I should give up on becoming a writer. (The letter was written by a fellow who, in his own way, also set me on my literary course.) There was a chance that Sheila's reply could have been as cruel as the guy from *New York Rocker*'s, but she wasn't capable of such venom or derision. She worked as closely with her young writers as with the veterans. She was also sage and prescient with her advice. The summer I went to study in Ireland, my band, the Rheostatics, was offered a tour of Northern Ontario. I was forced to choose between going to Trinity College in Dublin and playing bad country-and-western bars. I was torn between responsibility to myself and to my bandmates. One evening, I met Sheila downtown. After explaining my dilemma, she set me straight, exhorting, "Dave, please, go to Ireland!"

Sheila published my Devo story, then a bunch more. (I should mention that these stories weren't reviews but features. **Features** are longer stories that probe the greater aspects of a subject drawn out by interviews and other sources.) After a while, I asked Sheila if she wanted a story about the American band R.E.M. Like most good editors, she gave me the if-you-want-to-do-it-it's-good-enough-for-me seal of

approval. I warned her that the young band from
Georgia was elusive – lead singer Michael Stipe had
yet to grant a single interview to the Canadian music
press – but she decided to assign the piece anyway.

I have not been the best of reporters. I'm flawed
in the sense that I always turn back whenever sensitive subjects are raised by whomever I'm interview-
ing, perhaps as a reaction to having been asked
those kinds of invasive and difficult questions myself
while in my band. There are a lot of ways to
approach an interview. Some writers prepare long
lists of questions for their "subject" after exhaustive
research; others just start asking questions that
they've gathered in their head and follow the interview's path, sensing where to go as the subject opens
up and the conversation evolves. The best interviews
are conducted without a time limit, but often the
writer is resigned to a certain framework, and you've
got to work hard to get good answers before the
actor, musician, or athlete's time limit is exhausted.
During an early interview with New York punk
heroes the Ramones, I'd only asked six questions
before the record-company representative held up
two fingers: the two-minute warning. To make
matters worse, I'd forgotten to press the record

button on my tape recorder and retained none of their words. I called Sheila, who told me to write down everything that I could remember. I did, and the piece turned out fine.

I arrived at the R.E.M. show during sound check (being a musician, I knew that bands were most accessible – and vulnerable – at this point in their day and that the concert's security forces would not yet have mobilized). After playing a few songs, R.E.M. came down from the stage. Remarkably, so did singer Michael Stipe. I crossed the floor with my notebook in my hand and approached him. But as I did, another writer – a kid my age from a university paper – got to him first. I lingered behind him instead of pushing forward, eavesdropping on the conversation.

The writer ambushed Stipe with his questions. After a while, I could see that the singer was growing disenchanted; his answers got shorter, his voice quieter. I noticed pretty quickly that the writer's questions were inane and that, because Stipe wasn't responding, the writer had resorted to sensational queries, such as, "Have you ever met Robert Plant of Led Zeppelin?" Having prepared my opening question for weeks and, in a way, feeling bad that the singer had granted his first-ever Canadian interview only to be bombarded with nonsense, I stepped forward and asked, unflinchingly, if the heroine of one of R.E.M.'s songs had been inspired by Hester Prynne of Nathaniel Hawthorne's novel *The Scarlet Letter*. I followed this with a series of thoughts about why I suspected that she was. This is how Stipe responded:

"You know, it's not every day that I want some stranger coming up and giving me their opinions about a song, but to hear something like that is really refreshing."

I was thrilled. The interview continued without the other writer. It went so well that, at the end, I asked Stipe if he would pose for a photograph with the two of us with our backs to the camera, a request that my girlfriend had made from Italy, where she was taking a summer course. Stipe said that he would, and so we walked into the Toronto sunshine and stood beside R.E.M.'s silver-and-blue tour bus, where we officially documented our meeting.

Unfortunately *Shades* could only sustain itself for a few more years. By the time it **folded** (ceased to exist), I'd graduated to writing for other newspapers and magazines. But looking back at the names on the **masthead** (a box listing the names of owners and staff) of all of its other young writers, the common thread among us is that, twenty-five years later, almost everyone has stayed in the arts. No one ended up having to get a job working in a bank or car wash to sustain his or her interests. Paul Wilson became Czech writer Josef Skvorecky's noted translator; Elliott Lefko moved to California to promote huge concerts; Angela Baldassarre became a film critic and editor; Ron Gaskin managed bands and promoted experimental music shows; and the magazine's editor, Sheila Wawanash, went on to edit books for a living. For all of us, writing before we were very good at it gave way to better writing, which gave way to the kind of life we'd always wanted.

NATE AND HERMAN

One writer stereotype is that you are seemingly
awkward inside your own skin despite the wonderful
prose that pours out of you. *The Scarlet Letter*'s
author, Nathaniel Hawthorne, is one writer for
whom this stereotype fits. Hawthorne was a solitary
person until his marriage. He was a deep, aimless
brooder who only left his room to publish, which, at
age sixteen, consisted of a single story – "Solitude" –
a subject he knew all too well. On the other side of
the coin, *Moby-Dick*'s Herman Melville spent much
of his lively youth at sea, getting captured by cannibals after escaping a cruel captain, only to be rescued
four months later. (The cannibals, Melville reported,
had treated him quite well.)

DOYLE

After high school, I enrolled at York University, on
the northwest tip of Toronto proper. I was lucky to
have some great teachers. I was taught contemporary
English literature by Tess Hurson, a brilliant and
thoughtful woman from Northern Ireland, and
studied contemporary prose and poetry with a tall,
rumpled, and mischievous Englishman named Mr.
Girling (he never told us his first name). The first
thing he did after walking into the classroom was
write a profanity on the blackboard. Then he
explained about being in the war and how, because
he'd survived fighting in Europe, everything in life
was a bonus. I once presented an original poem in his
class that I credited to a fictional person, which
forced Mr. Girling to give me an unreadable book
about **semantics**, which is the branch of linguistics
concerned with the interpretation or meaning of
words. He passed it on gravely and told me to study

it with all of my life. But I couldn't get past the first few pages, and, a few weeks later, I admitted this. "Oh, I only gave you the book to upset you," he said, "to get you to work hard, so you never have to read this kind of stuff."

Another of my teachers was a fellow named Doyle. He was young, Irish, cool. He swore in class. He didn't suffer fools, but he didn't take anything too seriously. He'd originally moved to Canada to finish his graduate schooling but ended up spending more time watching bands. Other than the fact that he was brilliant and incisive, there was very little about him that was academic. Doyle destroyed my preconceptions about what the study of literature was all about. I looked forward to every one of his classes.

Once, we were required to attend a guest lecture about *Ragtime*, a book by American novelist E.L. Doctorow. The main thrust of the lecturer's presentation was that she'd been moved to tears by the book. "The pages were wet with tears by the end of it," she said, to which the crowd oohed and aahed its approval.

But something about the lecture struck me as phony and untrue. For me, university instructors were supposed to know how to articulate themselves, not fall prey to their emotions. Besides, crying over a book or a movie seemed like something a pre-teen might do, not a scholar, and the actual logistics of shedding enough tears to soak a page meant that the lecturer was probably ill, rather than simply moved. Either that, or she'd spilled a drink on the book. We'll never really know.

After the lecture, my classmates and I gathered in Doyle's classroom. He sat at the head of the class and asked what everyone thought of the lecture. A lot of the students said what they thought he wanted to hear, expressing how profoundly affected they'd been by the lecturer's confessional. This went on for five, ten minutes. Then, after everyone had exhausted themselves, Doyle looked wearily at the class and told us what we had to know:

"Well, I thought it was a piece of crap."

ZELDA AND F.

Doyle introduced me to American writers such as William Faulkner, F. Scott Fitzgerald, Stephen Crane, and others, all of whom you'll probably discover as you search out bigger, more important books. Doyle made them seem larger than life. I could have listened to stories about F. Scott Fitzgerald – who wrote *The Great Gatsby* in 1925 – and his wife, Zelda, all day long. Apart from the misery and alcoholism that eventually claimed them, they lived prank to prank to prank, with the odd bit of literary genius tossed in. Once, after being snubbed by movie producer Samuel Goldwyn in Hollywood, Zelda and F. showed up at Goldwyn's house, barking on their hands and knees until they were let in. Another time, after being ignored during their neighbors' dinner party, Zelda and F. threw bags of garbage on their patio in protest, and another time after that, they attended a tea where they collected a group of ladies' purses, boiled them in a pot, and served them as soup. Zelda liked to call the fire department regularly. When fire trucks showed up, she demanded that the fire fighters extinguish the blaze in her heart. Often, the Fitzgeralds would buy front-row tickets to the theater, only to burst out laughing in all the wrong places. Later, Zelda would tip the cab drivers to let her ride on the hood of the car. Zelda and F. were also infamous fountain jumpers, traveling from spout to spout across New York City, forging their wildness among the American literati.

THE WHEELBARROW

William Faulkner was one of F. Scott Fitzgerald's contemporaries. After getting his first book published in 1924, Faulkner took his advance and traveled to Europe, where he spent a year hopping trains, enjoying exotic food, and writing scads of material for what would become his first masterpiece, *The Sound and the Fury*. Arriving home from Europe, he was crestfallen to discover that, despite excellent reviews, his first book had made no money. Still, he persisted with his new work while writing and publishing three others, and eventually submitted *The Sound and the Fury* to his publishers. A few weeks later, he received a note telling him that they would publish it only if Faulkner consented to rewrite it completely.

His first impulse was to destroy the **manuscript** – which is what writers call a complete, unedited text – but for whatever reason, he resisted. Instead, he took a job as a night watchman and did as the publisher suggested, every night kneeling over an upturned wheelbarrow, which he used as a writing table. Rewritten and reimagined, the novel was accepted and is now regarded as one of the greatest achievements in modern American literature.

NATE WEST, WE THINK

William Faulkner ended up moving to Hollywood and working on screenplays – film scripts – for big movie studios. By all accounts, it was a lonely, sad life, even though there were buckets of cash to be made. Another American writer – Nathanael West – was responsible for one of the great Hollywood **novellas** (a smaller form of the novel) of his time, *The Day of the Locust*. West was a noted figure because of his reckless personality. After high school, he wanted desperately to get into college, but his marks were low. He found out that there was another Nate West in the area with excellent marks, so he pretended to be him and was granted admission. Another thing about West was that he was a terrible driver. As Ian Hamilton describes in *Writers in Hollywood*, West "was famous for day-dreaming at the wheel; several of his friends refused to drive with him. When 'bluntly warned' by one of them that 'some day he would be killed if he did not keep his eyes on the road,' his answer was always the same scornful laughter." But his friends' words proved prophetic. West died in a car crash in December 1940.

GARBAGE

It was Doyle's idea that I should study in Dublin, Ireland, which is where he was born and grew up. During my second last year at York, I applied – and was accepted – in an Anglo-Irish literature course at Trinity College, Dublin, though it's not as if I had to pass through a series of evaluations to make the grade. My old English literature professor, Tess, helped run the program, and as long as I sent a deposit – or, rather, my father did – they had room for me in the class.

In Ireland, I wrote a lot of garbage, but it's not what you think. Garbage helped me jump-start my literary life. I'm not being sarcastic, because a writer's garbage is beautiful and you have to learn to love it. Even though one's literary trash sometimes makes us want to hide our faces in embarrassment, a mountain of garbage has to pass before anything worthwhile is ever created. A few years ago, after my editor returned some old manuscripts that had been left at her office, she suggested that I donate them to a university. Then she reconsidered her position: "Maybe you better not let people see how much we had to take out to get these books published."

Here is some garbage:

In Dublin, I was encouraged to visit the *Book of Kells*, the age-old Celtic manuscript that was supposed to provide insight into Irish history and culture. It was located in one of Trinity's libraries, but despite the fact that it was only minutes from where I stayed, I never saw it. I was too busy pushing myself into the streets, discovering a whole new Dublin that would be my own.

There are a few reasons why this bit of writing is garbage. First, I axed it from this very book because, after reading it – and rereading it, then rereading it some more – I decided that you didn't need to know anything more, anecdotally, about my life in Dublin, let alone the *Book of Kells*, which has little importance to this narrative. Whenever I'm writing well – when I'm locked close to my thoughts – words spill over, and this passage is part of this spill, this creative mess. This might partly explain the passage's lazy imagery. After all, calling the *Book of Kells* "age-old" and "Celtic" is like calling *The Lord of the Rings* long and exciting. All told, the book you are now reading contained mountains of this narrative crud, which, after I restudied the text, were pushed to the back of the drawer to die a slow, literary death.

Most writers write badly before they write well. In the anthology *Writing Life*, Canadian author Margaret Atwood confesses to having written an unpublishable first novel yet finding satisfaction in the ability to start and finish a full-length work. Really, writing *anything* is valid and worthy of one's self-confidence because the mental effort it takes to commit to writing is taxing and time-consuming. At Trinity, I spent many glorious hours writing a bad novel about a kid hitchhiking across the United States. The writing was terrible. It stank. I still hate it. I am not reprinting it here because it's not even as good as "My Idol," which is really saying something.

Still, I can't help but think that "The Roaming Life of EJ Donnelly" (sounds pretty terrible, doesn't it?) led to more writing, which eventually led to my first book, which eventually led to the one you are reading now. This is partly because the process of writing my novel was never as painful as having to read it. I was endlessly inspired and energized looking out from my dorm-room window at the college's old cricket grounds, where people such as Irish writer Oscar Wilde had wandered in their day. The joy and satisfaction that I felt while writing was enough to make me realize that I wanted to do it a lot, possibly forever. That the work was junk is beyond the point. In fact, should any of you lay this book down to begin writing what ends up being a prize-winning first novel, you will be one of literature's great exceptions, but it doesn't really matter. What matters is whether the process is satisfying enough to make you want to write more. In the end, getting books published doesn't necessarily make you a writer, good or bad.

Writing does.

I remember suffering through parts of my second book, *Tropic of Hockey*, and grousing aloud about my creative frustrations to my friend, a musical composer, who reminded me about the importance of blue notes (flat musical notes that give blues its unique sound). He told me about Miles Davis, the great jazz trumpeter, and how he stressed that blue notes were as important as the others. "Art can't all be perfect," he said. "If it is, it isn't human. In music, especially, if there aren't any blue notes, there aren't any gold ones." This advice made me worry less about getting every word and paragraph perfect. I still sought perfection, but I tried not to get too hung up on it. If a sentence or passage wasn't working, I came back to it. Sometimes – but not always – those bits didn't seem as bad as when I'd first labored over them.

Not every brushstroke on an artist's canvas has to be perfect in order to create a startling image. With books, readers are engaged as much by the feel, ideas, enthusiasm, sensibility, intelligence, and honesty of a writer as they are by their command of language and clarity of thought. No writer should be dissuaded from putting pen to paper because they feel grammatically hamstrung: confused about where a semicolon goes, where to begin and end a paragraph, or whether to capitalize product names (we've all got *The Elements of Style* to help us with that). All young writers should know that without the creative learning curve, there would be no garbage, and without garbage, there would be no literature.

FANZINES

After coming home from Ireland, I started a fanzine
at York's radio station, University Radio York.
Whenever I meet young writers – especially those
with an interest in nonfiction arts writing – I tell
them to start a fanzine. Fanzines can be whatever
you want them to be. They're yours. You own, edit,
design, and write them. You are the god of your
fanzine, and nobody can tell you otherwise.

Fanzine describes a free or low-priced, photocopied, typewritten (at the time) magazine put
together mostly by young writers. There are more
fanzines now than ever. One of the reasons for this
post-punk explosion (fanzines entered the popular
consciousness in the late 1970s) is because fanzines
are an easy vehicle for anybody even remotely inter-
ested in making literature or publishing books.
Fanzines can be instructive in getting hands-on

experience in writing and publishing. Creating your own fanzine means learning about what a publication should look like and how it should sit in the reader's hands; editing for space, headline writing, and designing the look of the paper; how to sequence stories; what scissors can and can't do; what photo-copying shops are sensitive to the needs of a young fanziner; and what it feels like to spend an eternity producing something with all of your heart and soul only to have fifteen people read it, an experience that may or may not prepare you for the sometimes unap-preciated life of a professional writer. You'll also learn about the methods required to get your fanzine into as many hands as possible, which will prove valuable later on when you have to promote your first book.

My first fanzine was called *The Booth on the Roof*, which my friends and I produced from the offices of the campus radio station. We exploited the station's office supplies – glue, paper-cutter, assorted cardboard – to build it, but otherwise, most of the writing, transcribing, and typing happened at my parents' kitchen table. We had lots of fun putting *The Booth* together. I had friends write album reviews and other friends do the layout. Doyle contributed as well. He reviewed a China Crisis album and wrote other tidbits. Years later, he went on to write books and become a famous TV critic, for which I clearly deserve most of the credit.

POST-GARBAGE

After putting the failings of my cruddy novel behind me, I wrote a short story about a teenage hockey player. The story came easily because I wasn't trying too hard to write *The Greatest Story Ever Told*. A lot of young writers – myself included – set out to make their first book a work of epic genius, but, because we try too hard to achieve brilliance, good storytelling gets lost in the process. With my hockey story, I wrote for the heck of it, almost as if it were an exercise. After completing a first, second, then third draft, I used my "Young Sun" method and sent the unsolicited story – "Draft Day" – to a handful of literary journals.

THE STEPPING STONE

The world of the **literary journal** is shadowy and
hidden from a lot of young writers. These journals
exist like a handful of dwarf planets on the edge of
the publishing domain. The only way most folks find
out about them is whenever a stray copy of *Descant*,
The Antigonish Review, *Brick*, or *Queen's Quarterly*
happens to land on a shelf at the local library. Even
readers who live in big cities with decent magazine
shops are often required to search through the racks
for the latest *Granta*, *Fiddlehead*, or *Paris Review*.
Since the shape and design of the literary journal is
anomalous – they're generally square, palm-sized
books with cardstock covers and stiff spines – many
inexperienced shopkeepers have no idea what to do
with them. As a result, they tend to get shuffled
among *Tattoo'ed Dragster Illustrated* or *Protein
Supplement Weekly*, whose readers wouldn't know
a new Alice Munro story if it whacked them in the

chops. Then again, that literary journals are distributed at all in mag shops and bookstores is a huge step forward for a kind of publication that, for a long time, was about as hard to find as a frat joke in an *Anne of Green Gables* collection.

But to discover the world of the literary journal is – often – to put the writer on the next step (after writing for fanzines, magazines, and newspapers) toward full-fledged bookdom. Literary journals develop talent in the same way that coaches shape players' careers. Their editors are, traditionally, among the most sympathetic in the industry, and are more likely to take chances on unproven work than publishing houses, often giving life to voices too strong for the mainstream.

Some regionally conscious literary journals – such as *The Antigonish Review* in Nova Scotia – have fostered literature in their respective provinces (or states) for decades, bringing along generations of young voices that would otherwise have been forced to turn to distant outlets to get their words read. In particular, *The Fiddlehead* – Canada's oldest literary journal – has published early work by famous Canadian writers such as Al Purdy, Margaret Atwood, and Michael Ondaatje; really, anyone who is anyone in the CanLit galaxy. The same goes for

The Journey Prize Anthology, a collection of the best short fiction drawn from the year's literary journals and published since its inception by McClelland & Stewart, a Canadian publishing house.

To my astonishment and delight, "Draft Day" found a home at Kingston's *Quarry Press*, a small Southern Ontario literary journal. Reading it now, the story seems overwritten and self-conscious, but the letter I received from editor Steven Heighton (himself a Journey Prize alumnus) asking for permission to run it was the nearest thing to a message from the gods that I'd received in my short literary life. As you know – or as you'll soon discover – submitting a story **blind** (without being asked) is like bear hunting with a lawn dart, so whenever a submission brings back positive words and the promise of publication, it provides endless fuel for a writer's self-confidence and ego. After hearing from Heighton, I felt as if I was being punted toward a distinguished career as a Canadian novelist (that I decided to pursue mostly a life in nonfiction should be no reflection on Heighton's kindness), and when I received a copy of the small journal in the mail, running my fingers across the embossed BIDINI printed next to a list of writers I'd never heard of – but who sounded important – it was one of the great tactile experiences of my life. Seeing one's name in print is always a thrill, but having it inlaid on fine, textured paper gives it permanence, as if it was somehow meant to be there.

DIRTY LAUNDRY

After my days at York University, I kept writing
about music and sports for various newspapers and
magazines. Then, in 1991, I landed a job writing a
weekly column (about seven hundred words) for the
Toronto Star's "Weekend" section. I'd previously
written for a local entertainment paper called
Metropolis, and my work had been noticed by Craig
McInnis, an editor with the *Star* and another in a
long line of literary types who was unreasonably
kind and helpful to me.

It goes without saying that writing for Canada's
largest newspaper was a big deal. It was the greatest
platform I'd ever had for my writing, but I found the
whole process achingly trying. Writing a weekly
column was different because it meant that I had to
have fresh, interesting ideas about life and culture
ready four times a month. There's a real art to writing

a column, because its word count limits one's abilities to explore a concept or subject in a small amount of space. At journalism schools such as Ryerson University in Toronto or Carleton University in Ottawa, entire classes are devoted to being precise, funny, and wise within these limitations, but because I hadn't much experience writing a column, I learned on the job. In the past, I'd had months to get my words right, but now I had only days.

The size of the newspaper's readership started to play on my self-confidence to the point that I ended up putting too much pressure on myself to create prize-winning prose and less time just writing. Long were the hours that I walked the streets rapping my head with my fists trying to think of great ideas when I should have been pulling stories from everyday life and writing about what I saw and how I felt. My voice became muffled, and my writing lost its sense of fun. I suppose I had momentary fits of creativity, but I spent too much time trying to prove that I could write well and not enough time just writing. But because writing for the *Star* was a huge opportunity to establish a wide readership, I wanted badly to impress. There were occasions when I found myself with less than twenty-four hours to come up with an

idea for my column, only to stare for hours at my
computer screen wondering whether the size of my
laundry pile might make for compelling reading.
Worse, I sometimes decided that it did.

THE AXE

I was fired from my job at the *Star*, which wasn't as bad as it sounds. It was a soft firing – the paper was eliminating the "Weekend" section altogether and moving its editor – Peter Goddard, who'd tried to teach me the form – to another section. My new editor told me that if I wanted to continue to write, I could, although my picture would no longer appear next to my **byline** (a line giving the writer's name). This was disturbing news because I'd always thought that my picture was one of the better parts of the column. Still, losing the gig was a blessing. Not having to write every week turned out to be a creative relief.

LUCK

I know there are countless stories of writers persevering in the face of misery and failure, but, as Ms. Atwood has stressed, luck plays a large part in a writer's career. In the sporting world, there are three things that scouts mention when they talk about what gets a player to the major leagues: hard work, talent, and luck. It's no different in writing. Writers and athletes have never been denied success on the basis of their looks, but countless actors have been turned away because they were too short, too strange, too fat. But you can't cheat at writing or playing goal in the NHL. History has shown that very few writers/athletes have backdoored their way to fame and fortune.

Okay: luck. After getting dumped by the *Star*, I met Paul Quarrington, the great Canadian novelist/humorist/musician who, legend has it, wrote his first novel on an overturned hotel drawer while touring with his blues band, Joe Hall and the Continental Drift. In 1992, my band, the Rheostatics, wanted to name our new record after one of Paul's books (*Whale Music*), so we met him to ask permission, which he granted. A little while later, Paul was hired to edit a book of hockey stories, and he thought of me. Fortunately, the person who'd hired Paul for the job was my old editor at the *Star*, Peter Goddard, who also wanted my writing to be part of the collection.

I escaped to my apartment and wrote a story based on the life of the old Chicago Blackhawks goalie Charlie Gardiner. Everyone liked the story, and when the book came out, the reviews were good. The unofficial launch of the book was held at the McClelland & Stewart offices (they shared a space with Reed Books, who published Paul's *Original Six: True Stories from Hockey's Classic Era*), and it was the first time I'd ever stepped foot inside a real publishing house.

A few weeks later, I received a phone call from Paul's literary agent, David Johnston, who asked if I had any book ideas. I had lots. He told me to write them down, then we'd meet to talk turkey.

THE PRINCE OF DARKNESS

Okay: agents. There never used to be a demand for agents in Canadian publishing because few people were submitting **unsolicited** (not asked for) manuscripts with the intent to publish. Aspiring authors would send off their pages and editors would read them and reply positively, or not. But in 2007, most young – or unestablished – writers won't get their work noticed unless they have **representation**, meaning an agent.

I realize, at this point, that you're expecting me to deliver suggestions, or instructions, on how to acquire an agent, but I can't tell you much more than the basics. Get one of those publishing how-to books, where agents are listed and rated. This is lame advice, I know, but it's the best I can do. It was really nothing more than dumb luck that Dave Johnston contacted me, because I wouldn't have known the first thing about approaching an agent. In fact, asking writers to

persuade agents to represent them is a little like asking
a librarian to audition for the lead role in a Broadway
musical. (Note: Although I am aware that there are
many musically gifted librarians out there, I'm trying
to illuminate the shy writer's plight by using the diffi-
culties inherent in moving from one of the world's
quietest, most hushed jobs to the world's most bom-
bastic. I have nothing but respect and admiration for
book-minders, and expect little recrimination.)

Because writers don't have to be socially persua-
sive to be good at their jobs – and because so much
of our time is spent quietly pecking at our work
alone, in a most non-social environment – it's not
part of our skill set to convince strangers to help
further our careers. Writing is such an insecure
endeavor anyway – art, in general, is insecure, even
though actors and musicians spend more time than
writers sharing their art with large groups of people
– that asking a writer to win the faith of an agent is
an unreasonable task.

Still, it's something that has to be done. In many
towns, there are writers' groups that probably have a
better sense than the young writer about how to go
about winning an agent (or finding a publisher). In
some cases, these micro-communities might even
include the occasional agent, publisher, or editor who

can be useful in helping the young writer take that next step from late-night scratcher to published author. Literary types are also likely to congregate at readings, book launches, or literary festivals, and there's nothing holding the young writer back from, at best, meeting them and picking their brains. Because there's a lot less money in books than there is in, say, movies or rock and roll, the literary ego tends to be less exaggerated, and competitiveness among publishers and writers is minimal. Writing people are, generally, a lot nicer too, making them far less likely to swat away your manuscript the way a recording company might reject a young band's demo, or a studio executive might upbraid a young director trying to sell a movie project.

The first idea I presented to Dave Johnston – who favored black turtlenecks and was nicknamed the Prince of Darkness by Paul Quarrington – was a book about my band's tour with The Tragically Hip. It was based, mostly, on a newspaper story – a tour diary – that I'd written for the *Toronto Star*. The article became my proposal, more or less. Dave sent it out and there was some interest. Three or four publishers called back, McClelland & Stewart among them.

I was wary of M&S because I'd signed a recording deal a few years before with Sire Records, which had gone sour. (Perhaps "sour" is the wrong way of putting it. Rather, we withered on the vine from lack of company interest.) I wanted to sign with Sire because it was the company that had put out the favorite albums of my youth, and M&S was the literary equivalent of this, having published almost every book I'd read in middle school. I decided that nostalgia was the wrong basis upon which to make a decision, so I waited to see how things would play out.

In the end, M&S proved to be the most attractive publisher, but nothing was decided. A few days later, I was out celebrating my wife's birthday with her family at a restaurant on Elm Street in Toronto when I received a cell-phone call from my agent: M&S had offered $25,000 for my book, which was more money than I'd earned in my entire life. Needless to say, I was over the moon. I returned to the table and told my in-laws that I was going to take the M&S offer, at which point my father-in-law said, "Great. Now, if you can only do that four times a year, you'll be okay."

THE WRITER'S BARK

Every writer has their personal tools of destruction:
pen, quill, computer, notebook. William Golding
wrote *Lord of the Flies* entirely in school exercise
books. Jack Kerouac wrote *On the Road* on one
continuous scroll. For me, I started writing, in
earnest, with a blue-ink V-Point pen in a Pro Art
artist's sketchbook. These books ended up containing the bulk of *On a Cold Road* and subsequent
works. Generally, I write in my Pro Art first, then
later transcribe my words – provided I can decipher
them – into a Mac laptop, which I bought second-
hand from a local tech shop. I buy my pens twelve
to a box because I tend to lose a lot of them, fitting,
as they do, between sewer grates, under seat cushions, and behind heaters. The books, however, I buy
only one at a time. Purchasing two in a single stop
means you're expected to fill up both, which, even

for the most prolific writer, is presumptuous and fate-tempting.

I'd recommend these sketchbooks for a few reasons. First, the paper stock is substantial. I've always felt that paper found in those cheap spiral notebooks lacks a certain permanence. The act of writing, to me, feels otherwise transient unless the ink is soaked into high-quality paper that can only be torn from its binding with severe tugging. And because my Pro Art sketchbooks are, essentially, artist's paper, my scribbles tend to look good on the parchment (American novelist Paul Auster – who prefers lined notebooks – has likened prose entered in these kinds of books to "a house of words"). My sketchbooks are hardcover and black, with paper that yields a busy, scratchy sound, the sound of someone working, which is a notion that most writers need reinforced lest they feel guilty for doing something they love while everyone else is out selling shirts or building highways (Benjamin Cheever has written that he remembers his father's work – American novelist John Cheever – as a sound: a machine-gun rattle that resulted from countless assaults on the keyboard). When closed, my sketchbook possesses almost a hushed power. While loose notebooks or spiral pads

Emotionalism, part 114: From John Olerud's natural field line-run against Scott Bankes in the 7th inning of the last game in mid-season vs. Caltown to Martin Tielli's effortless guitar solo in the middle section of things to Dave Allen laughs at my stupid jokes to Don't Look Back to a pretty girl in a red dress, my brain is replete with blood and my heart finds a boom - boom - boom like the joy, throbbing ether - hoof of life, and back by Charlie. Despite the ever-confusing and abstract lines of numbwood, things are rippled in the singlest ways - being passed half-open windows; keep cool, fingers the keyhole. Little-League alcoholism runs viewpoint, yet the writer will - no, must - hold it as we once traverse the big bopping once again. Remorse may be the center of existence, but it's not enough, as Charlie masks. Life is too full of distractions to ignore one for the other. I will do radio + continue to write in spite of his romantic, egocentric born sandy devisoral to all this rock n' roll. Like sitting on the steps of the Blue Jays dugout doing batting practice: how could you compensate for that in a 3-chord moment at an empty club in your hometown? Vice versa, I suppose. We live in a sea of dreams. Like clutching crowdos into a ball - one box - while size or sour are really loud and far then to occupy colours, lord? I dunno. Six-seeks wide? I hope not. No chance to dig into the intricate, and that sex, you know? Oh well, don't explain so much. Tom Lewless livens. thanks to Tom, thanks to Bill Payne ...

· Ⓧ ·

invite being flipped open, I'd like to think that if an interloper drew back the cover of my sketchbook, a deadly tongue of smoke would shoot from its binding, protecting my almost-words.

Another reason I favor the Pro Art sketchbook is because, whenever I'm traveling, I like to collect tokens from my visit that will help me later to evoke what it was like to be traveling abroad. The Pro Art paper is the perfect canvas for gluing candy wrappers, bus transfers, concert tickets, street pamphlets, show announcements, and newspaper clippings. These tokens help me remember my trip and are particularly valuable in case I end up documenting the experience later.

MY BUTCHER

I've titled this section – about my editor, Dinah Forbes – half-jokingly, because her successive attempts to prune my manuscripts have been largely done with intelligence and sensitivity, as opposed to slash-and-burn rage. Which isn't to say that she hasn't slashed and burned. She has, but only with deep care and affection for the work.

One of the main challenges for a writer is to open themselves to another person who is as responsible for the finished manuscript as the writer. This isn't easy. After spending years, sometimes decades, on a manuscript, the writer becomes so invested in the work that it is held aloft, as if it were a figure cut from marble or a precious antique vase. Often, it's the editor's job to take that vase, place it in the middle of the table, and smash it to bits with a ball-peen hammer.

I was horrified the first time I saw the marked-up

manuscript for *On a Cold Road*. It looked like a child had scribbled over it with great disrespect. My entire first paragraph, which, I felt, had taken thirty-five years to write, had arrows shooting through words and blotches of pencil smeared across what amounted to my life's work. Going into our editing session, I expected a tuck here, a nip there, a sentence or two pushed about, but, to my horror, entire blocks of prose had been removed. Worse, Dinah smiled through the carnage and said, confidently, that it was all for the best.

It takes a while to learn that when an editor insists that a passage or section of a book doesn't work, he or she isn't trying to slice down your literary aspirations at the ankles but, in fact, is balancing the work as a whole. Because my first editing session lasted one week, I became worn-out from having to fight for every single word. In the end, I picked my battles. The book came out and people liked it. Every editing session afterward got a little easier because there was acknowledgment on both sides – but mostly from my side – that being edited was, ultimately, a good thing.

On the next page is the beginning of *On a Cold Road* after Dinah's editorial savagery. See the legend for an explanation of the editorial markup.

"Zero degrees is where we start."
Max Webster, "In Context of the Moon"

I was nothing but a pimply little question mark on the day that I walked into Ken Jones Music in Etobicoke, where an unclean fellow in a long shawl sat behind the counter holding a mandolin. Sunlight streamed through the windows, and dappled the guitars that hanged behind him like Byzantine swords, bathing the small music shop at the back of the Westway Plaza in warm light. The store was cluttered with drums stacked on top of each other, glinting keyboards leaning three deep against the walls, dusty racks of unread sheet music, long out-dated band want-ads taped to the cash register, and ashtrays scattered across old chairs and window ledges. At the back of the store, young boys sat in tiny rooms plucking guitars through amplifiers that buzzed like heat bugs, the sound of their hammer-ons and finger-rolls and string-benders snaking out under doors to where I sat with my hands in my lap, sucking it all in like sugar through a pixie-stik.

After tasting this place for the first time, my sister and I signed up for guitar lessons, which I grew to hate. My disdain might have had something to do with the fact that she mastered basic chords and strumming before I'd grown my first finger callous. She out-licked me on "Kumbaya," "Michael Row the Boat Ashore," and "House of the Rising Sun," which we debuted for our parents in our living room on bridge-table chairs with music stands in front of us. I'd like to tell you that I rose to her challenge and went on to become a blurry-fingered virtuoso of the fretboard whose technique set the world's pants on fire. But I did not.

Editor's Markup

⌇	Delete	⟳	Transpose
◡	Close up; delete space	(ital)	Set in italic type
⟳	Delete and close up (use only when deleting letters within a word)	(rom)	Set in roman type
#	Insert space	cap (caps)	Set in capital letters
[	Move left	∧	Insert here
(fl)	Flush left	⌄	Insert comma
		⊙	Insert period

A IS FOR ATWOOD

Margaret Atwood is probably Canada's best-known writer. When one thinks of CanLit, one thinks of her. Ms. Atwood has very small hands; I know this because I shook one of them and, to quote my wife, it was like holding a small bird. Our encounter came during a soiree held by my new publisher, who is also Ms. Atwood's, at the Art Gallery of Ontario. Waiters worked the room carrying trays with little sandwiches and glasses of champagne, and I saw my new book on a display next to Ms. Atwood's, which probably meant that I was CanLit too. Somewhere, I hoped that Mr. Romkema felt vindicated.

Publishers portend to publish, but what they really do is worry about whether the general public will wake up one day and realize the folly and insignificance of making books when it seems far more practical to spend time and money paving roads and designing smaller telephones. The publishing business, it seems, is forever hanging by a thread because, unlike other mass entertainments, buying and reading and spending time with books is to forge a deep and time-consuming relationship with authors and their words, which is to say, a heckuva lot of trouble. Of course, it's also deeply rewarding, but in the twenty-first century, it seems that fewer people are inclined to read. Instead, a lot of folks want what they can get fast: swallowing a television show in thirty minutes, stepping in and out of a video game that they can stop and start, and sampling pop ditties on iPods. But with books, it's page to page to page. Publishers cringe every time a speedy new techno-entertainment seizes the public imagination, because our habits as consumers of art and other diversions change.

That said, publishers are generally pretty noble types, and they're excused if they sometimes act this way. Publishers run publishing houses, and when I first hooked up with M&S, my publisher was a fellow named Douglas Gibson, who is on speaking terms, it seems, with every Canadian who ever wrote a book. I liked Mr. Gibson – he's a tall, tweedy gentleman with a mile-long look in his eyes – because he told colorful stories about famous writers. Hearing them firsthand, I felt closer to those writers – such as W.O. Mitchell and Jack Hodgins – whom I'd read as a kid. Once, Mr. Gibson told me about the time that W.O. got stung on his crotch by a bumblebee, after which the prairie writer seemed to me less famous than he had before and a little more like you and me. Mr. Gibson had the ability to erase the line between his publishing house's most famous authors and those who wrote books about wine and gardening (or rock and roll and hockey), understanding that no matter how many more books one writer sells than the next, we all suffer through the same kind of ordeal to get our words out.

After the publication of *On a Cold Road*, I was struck with the sobering thought that I might not ever write another book. (This thought strikes almost every writer who's ever finished a book.) Then, at the Canadian Booksellers Association convention (now called BookExpo Canada) – a Toronto gathering each June where publishing houses hype their fall books to visiting booksellers from across Canada – Mr. Gibson asked me, "So what do you plan to write about next?" I told him I was thinking of going around the world to play hockey. He said it was a great idea and that M&S would like to publish that book too.

SEVEN FRILLY PILLOWS

Writers love literary festivals – also known as writers'
festivals – not only because we get paid to read from
something we've already been paid to write but
because of the effect our work has on a live audience.
It's always a delicious moment when you look into a
crowd and spy a person attending their first festival,
someone who can't believe how much fun they're
having. Expectations among first-time literary atten-
dees are, understandably, quite low. After all, it's
hard to imagine how listening to an introverted
writer who spends much of his or her time alone in a
small room read from a long and involved literary
work might possess any energy or excitement. But,
in fact, readings can be among the most gripping and
intimate of all entertainments. Coming from a background of crash cymbals and Marshall stacks, I can
tell you that reading in low light from a modest
podium affords the performer little to hide behind:

no drum solo, no moving backdrop, no fuzz wah. It's among the most naked of all performances. On the other hand, it's not like the writer is required to invent on the spot or struggle to memorize his lines. Reading is what most of us do hundreds of times a day anyway, only, at a literary festival, it's done in public, in front of lots of people. This, of course, is a scenario that terrorizes many writers, but I'm always surprised when mousy men and women who would probably struggle to say five words to you in an elevator take the stage and emote, reading from passages they've labored over for years and got right for purposes such as this.

Another reason why writers love literary festivals is because it spares them having to do reading and promotional tours. Personally, I've never found the literary road very grueling compared to what I've gone through traveling with my band, but the experience is always mixed. Small crowds often show up at promising events, while great nights can arise out of nothing. Paul Quarrington once told me that he and best-selling author Wayne Johnston drove for five hours to Windsor – a boring, mind-numbing highway drive – for a book signing attended by no one. I heard this story while suffering through an eerily similar experience with Paul at a bookstore in

Calgary, where we were promoting *Original Six*. We were seated at a little table with stacks of books between us when finally a woman – a former student of Paul's – showed up. She sat down and we drew our pens in hopes of signing (and selling) a book, but it turned out that she wasn't in the mood to shop, or to talk much either.

Writer Matt Cohen was once invited to read at an out-of-province university in the winter. He flew into town, took a taxi to the school, and went searching through the cold campus for the location of the reading. Of course, he found no signs or advertisements for the event but for a single piece of paper on the door of a lecture hall, announcing that the reading had been moved to a nearby classroom. When he got there, one person sat waiting for his reading. He suggested to the fellow that they adjourn to one of the campus bars and have a conversation, but the fellow demanded, rather intractably, that Cohen honor his commitment and read. After he finished, the lone attendee said nothing and left. It was only moments after he'd gone that Matt realized he had no way of getting off campus, so he went racing after his "fan," whom he found getting into his car, firing his engine, and promptly leaving.

Bill Gaston, the acclaimed writer/poet/teacher, told me that one time, as part of a book tour, he was scheduled to read on the college campus in Salmon Arm, British Columbia. Bill said, "The host/organizer had been really sick with the flu, so sick that he didn't put up any posters, or notices in the paper or on radio, or even greet me the evening of the event. I was all alone in this classroom, until a woman poked her head in. She was lost and asked me where the yoga class was. I didn't know, so, frustrated, she sat down and caught her breath. We chatted. Her name was Vera. I asked if she wanted to hear a story and she somewhat suspiciously, or politely, said, 'Okay.' I read Vera a story, the funniest in my collection, and after I told her it was all right to laugh, she laughed a few times. She stayed for the whole story, never looking all that comfy, and left when it was done. She didn't know what a literary reading was, and she might have thought I was insane and in some vague way holding her captive. She might not have been wrong on either count.

"Another time, I read at Harbourfront, in Toronto, with an author from the States. He'd just won the Pulitzer Prize. He was an egomaniac, in any case, and this prize seemed to have made him worse.

At the pre-reading dinner, the host asked us both not to go over our allotted thirty minutes, please, because 'the mind cannot hold what the bum cannot stand,' or something like that. The writer said nothing very loudly for a minute and squeezed his wineglass stem so hard that his fingertips went white. He said, to the table, a comma between each word, 'When, I, start, reading, no, one, will, want, to, be, anywhere, else.' Anyway, his reading sucked, his stuff was boring, and mine, I thought (not to be an egomaniac) was pretty good. But everyone had paid to see him and at the book-buying and signing table, he had a lineup stretching all the way around the corner. Me, I had someone (who looked a bit like Vera) come up and ask me if I knew where the bathroom was. I didn't sell or sign a book. I waited maybe three minutes for my personal Beatlemania to begin, but it didn't, and I fled, humbled into the dark night. The possibility that I sucked, and not him, still has not arisen in my mind."

Despite the occasional sour episode, homegrown writers are fortunate that, in Canada, there are many great and esteemed literary festivals. Here, writers are given a chance to meet other like-minded authors, as well as be rewarded for their work with a weekend of relatively high living. Once, after arriving at my hotel for WordFest – Calgary's annual literary festival – I found a giftwrapped package sitting on the bed. I approached the flowered box with great trepidation – Was it a bomb? Some kind of ironic joke? Was I in someone else's room? To my delight, the box contained a handsome leather saddlebag with WORD-FEST sewn on the side, both allaying my fears and suspicions, and leaving me disappointed whenever subsequent literary festivals provided nothing more than a modest honorarium.

Another time, I showed up for the Vancouver International Writers Festival – one of the great literary festivals of the world – to find out that I'd been prechecked into the Granville Island Hotel. After getting my room key, the desk clerk told me, "Mr. Bidini, you have a very nice room." Surprised – and grateful – that the person who'd called me Mr. Bidini wasn't working for any of the local police forces, I rode the elevator to the fourth floor to discover that my "nice" room was, in fact, a penthouse apartment, with a hot tub in the bedroom and a balcony overlooking the Granville Island marina. Convinced that there'd been some kind of a mistake, I phoned the desk clerk and told him that it was all too much, at which point he imparted the second-best piece of advice I've ever been given regarding the literary road racket: "Never turn down a nice room." (The best piece of advice had come previously from Paul Quarrington, who told me, "When on a publisher-sponsored reading tour, always order room service.") Bewildered by the extravagance of these palatial digs, I flopped down on my frilly seven-pillowed bed and ordered room service. I phoned my wife and told her that I had a hot tub in my room, then called her back to tell her about the pillows. After the second call, she advised me not to call her again. I said that I'd try, then blasted open the taps on the tub and uncorked the room's complimentary bottle of champagne, savoring, if for a moment, a world where the Canadian writer is king and his literary achievements are celebrated with seven frilly pillows.

THE MIRACLE OF ROME

A lot is made of where a writer writes and what it takes, setting-wise, to get a writer in the proper head-space so that he or she can work. But where one writes is not necessarily related to what or how one writes. There's a certain belief among some writers that sitting in a wood-paneled room sucking fresh country air through a window overlooking open fields or majestic fjords is a sure-fire recipe for literary gold, but you could be floating on a cloud nibbling grapes and still the words might not come. And because very few of us have access to a field or fjord – and assuming that your teenage writing space is probably more like a shoe trunk than a cabin, located in a room between your sister's and your parents' – writers more or less have to make do with whatever cube we're stuffed into. This has created a demand for writers' retreats, which offer fantasy writing environments where scribes can hide away in hopes of finding the muse.

This environment might be fine for some, but I don't think it's for me. This is not to discredit entirely the concept – being in a beautiful setting rife with natural stimuli and *not* writing actually sounds like a pretty sweet deal – but I believe that a writer should be able to write while settled in a cold ditch with a rock for a desk. Besides, were I forced into a literary idyll, I'd feel too pressured to write, and to write well. I can't imagine what it might do for my self-esteem if, after spending two weeks in the great wilderness, all I ended up with was pencil burn and bad ideas. This might explain why I tend to write easily in places busy with sound and people – cafés, mostly – and why I need just enough noise and distraction to work.

While living in Havana, American novelist Ernest Hemingway prepared a workroom in his home, but he rarely used it. Instead, he wrote in his bedroom, using the top of a bookcase for a table (Hemingway wrote standing up). When a writer from *The Paris Review* was dispatched to interview him, he described a massive flattop desk sitting unused in the bedroom. Hemingway was crammed into "a square foot . . . hemmed in by books on one side and . . . a newspaper-covered heap of papers, manuscripts, and pamphlets [with] just enough space left on top of the bookcase for a typewriter."

If I've learned anything as a relatively seasoned scribbler, it's the importance of writing at all costs, no matter what the circumstances, whether you find yourself in a groove or not. Not only will this help you establish a disciplined approach to your craft, but a writing routine tends to make you feel like a real writer, even if you're not yet published. That said, while it's good to write when the mood isn't striking, it's even better to write when it is. Since precious are the moments when writing feels effortless, it's important to ride one's wave of inspiration at all costs. Poet Robert Frost has described writing on the bottom of his shoe while riding a train. Toni Morrison has talked about searching for a certain phrase or sentence and what she does to capture it the moment it "arrives," reaching for a subway transfer, the margins of a business card, exposed skin, bits of newspaper, dry-cleaning tickets, serviettes, and whatever other kinds of parchment may be at hand to engrave one's thoughts and keep these rare and glorious moments alive.

Once, while writing my third book, *Baseballissimo*, I was brought to a soccer match in Rome by my

friend Mario. I'd wanted to write about soccer –
"football" in Europe – because of the passion of the
Italian fans, and as we made our way inside the
howling bowl of Stadio Olimpico, the scene was
everything I had been promised and more: eighty
thousand wild S.S. Lazio fans singing and pounding
drums. Before going to the game, I knew that Mario
was a supporter of the visiting team, A.C. Milan;
what I didn't know was that I'd be sitting in a tiny
wedge of the stadium with other Milanese support-
ers, penned in by Plexiglas walls to protect us from
the S.S. Lazio fans, who threw themselves at our bar-
ricades and hurled batteries, mandarin oranges,
coins, and other projectiles over the walls.

At the start of the game, red flares flew out of the
crowd and smoke gathered over the field as an enor-
mous eagle flag – S.S. Lazio's totem – unfurled over
the northern section of the arena. I rushed to docu-
ment all that I was seeing, only to discover that I'd
forgotten my sketchbook and pen in the car. I feared
that I couldn't possibly remember all that I was
seeing – of course, I probably could have had I not
been absorbed by so much self-doubt – so I searched
my jean jacket for paper and anything resembling a
crude writing device.

I came up with a set of keys and a religious prayer card I'd taken from a church. My first notion was that I'd try to engrave a few impressions into the card using the key, but when I did, I discovered that the key could actually write, if only in a clunky gray script on a piece of paper no bigger than a postcard. Looking to the skies, I felt blessed by St. Francis de Sales – the patron saint of writers – and began driving the key feverishly into the paper, recording everything that was going on. During the game, I was convinced that I'd been the benefactor of a kind of literary miracle, but that's where *Baseballissimo*'s divine intervention began and ended. Upon publication, the book was panned in two national newspapers and failed to secure the five-figure U.S. publishing deal that everyone had anticipated.

CRITICS

The critics – or reviewers – liked my first two books.
And then there was *Baseballissimo*. After a succes-
sion of praise, I was carved up for my Italian baseball
story. Other than the fact that this made me question
my abilities as a writer and the general validity of the
book, two reviews – one in the *Globe*, another in the
National Post (the *Star*, thank goodness, liked it) –
proved complicated in other ways.

The editor of the *Globe and Mail* book section is
a fellow named Martin Levin. For Canadian
readers, the *Globe*'s book section, which appears
every Saturday, can be useful in terms of knowing
what new books are coming out, who's publishing
them, and what kinds of books are getting the
attention of the critics, for better or for worse. The
Globe also provides a forum where local readings
are announced, so it's a good way – along with
Canada's national literary monthly, *Quill & Quire* –

to keep abreast of which famous writers might be passing through town.

When I was twenty-two years old, I was a **stringer** (freelance reporter) for Martin Levin's national baseball magazine, *Innings*. It wasn't Martin's intent, I don't think, to pass my book on to a reviewer for slicing and dicing – hoping, instead, for a fair perspective – but that's what happened. I was crestfallen, and I think he was too. Worse, the review came out on a weekend when all of my friends and peers were amassed at a huge regional hockey tournament. Walking into the rink that weekend, I tried not to notice the number of people reading the Saturday *Globe*, in part because I didn't want to know and, in part, because there were simply too many copies of the papers lying around to count.

Baseballissimo's other negative review was written by someone I'd known but had never met: a good friend of a friend of a friend. It raised the question of why, or how, reviewers are able to write awful things about people with whom they share a community. It's a question that can be answered only by the reviewer, but personally, I'd long ago stopped writing reviews after experiencing what it was like to be reviewed negatively. I didn't want to inflict the kind of pain or self-doubt on others that had been inflicted on me, and this weakened my ability as a reviewer. The best kinds of critics are smart, eloquent but, most of all, dispassionate. They can judge a book on its merit alone – or lack thereof – and feel little in the way of guilt, or fulfillment, after panning or triumphing the work.

WISE WORDS

Another way that young writers can learn about the lives of other writers and their books is through the literary interview. The maven of the literary interview is a woman named Eleanor Wachtel, who hosts a weekly CBC Radio program called *Writers & Company*. While I've tried to pass sage advice on to you through these pages, you can glean as much writerly wisdom and direction from her interviews as you can from this book. Since authors very rarely get asked to discuss their work outside of literary festivals or occasional book tours, the conversations between Eleanor and her subjects are rich in detail and insight.

Another source for firsthand knowledge of the writing racket is the most famous of all literary journals, *The Paris Review*. Every issue features one or two full-length interviews with writers. The questions are often mailed (or e-mailed) so that the writers can compose and consider their responses. The writers' answers are great and eloquent, and a treat to read and reread when seeking advice from the best.

The Believer is another monthly magazine that devotes a lot of time to authors. For a few years, British novelist Nick Hornby (author of *High Fidelity*, which was later made into a successful Hollywood film starring John Cusack) wrote a wonderful column that discussed the books he was reading – or, often, not reading. A few years ago, these articles were collected as *The Polysyllabic Spree*, which also comes highly recommended.

GREEN IS GREEN

There are a few dozen writers in Canada – perhaps it's not even that big a number – who exist solely by writing novels or nonfiction books every few years. Making art in Canada is often about compensating your existence by working in a variety of capacities and hoping that your supplementary work supports that which you have dreamed of doing since you were a small child. I've largely neglected to discuss money or income here, in a way because it's a depressing topic and, in a way, because money tends to besmirch and distort that great and noble pursuit of art. Then again, very few writers' lives can be revealed without discussing the litany of menial jobs that they did in order to pay the bills so they could spend time tapping deep into their souls to write prose that blossoms on the page. That I never had to clean the insides of oil tankers or slaughter chickens or sell stereos does not suggest that other writers haven't had to. Somehow, I am the exception: lucky, and blessed with personal support and good fortune.

Despite these less-than-ideal circumstances, every author has their own reasons for returning to the tablet. In *Writing Life* – I keep referring to this collection, published in 2006 by M&S, because of its depth and excellence, and seeing as you've already purchased my, uh, deep and excellent book, you should purchase this title next – author Marilyn Bowering talks about the isolation of the writer and wonders why any writing happens at all when "many books are never read beyond the narrowest of circles. . . . A work may have the potential to inform and enlighten thousands – but that audience, for that writer, [often] remains beyond reach." She cites a handful of times when people have asked her why she does what she does though her work affects a relatively small number of people. She explains how, when a writer writes, his or her audience is the furthest thing from the writer's mind.

In my case, being in an alternative Canadian rock band was excellent preparation for the vacuum of CanLit. In fact, even though hundreds of thousands of readers have yet to alight upon my work so that I might be provided with endless cash flow and sustained self-worth, I've always sold more books than the band sold albums, and small triumphs are writ large in my author's life. Once, a friend who was entrusted with adapting my first book for television hired a researcher who'd yet to read the book. She borrowed it from her local library, and when she brought it to a meeting to discuss the project, I saw that the book was decimated, its covers nearly ripped off. When I suggested that she take better care of something that was hers only temporarily, she laughed and told me that she'd found it this way on the shelf: bent, clawed, devoured, and nearly destroyed by its readers.

Because writing is an unconventional job, I've never thought of it as real work, certainly not the kind of work done by my father, his father, or his father's father. Even though it requires the same kind of sweat and blood and pain and anxiety as any other job, what I produce is largely ethereal because, in the end, it's measured by how it affects other people. Unless you can see the cat-clawed text in front of you, you'll never really know. A writer has to have faith that what he or she is creating is working in the greater world, that it's communicating despite the fact that literature, especially poetry, can't hold a candle to DVD or video-game sales. For some writers, good and bad, even the laurels are never enough. When my wife told me that *Tropic of Hockey* had been named one of M&S's one hundred best titles of the century, my response was, "Well, *On a Cold Road* was pretty darned good too!"

Ultimately, the writer has to find solace in the small rewards. Because my parents' generation wanted their kids to become doctors, lawyers, accountants, dentists, generals, nurses, and NHLers, there was always something about becoming a writer (and a musician) that seemed less respectful or serious or proper or secure than what everyone else did, something less professional, less real. So I have tried to draw strength from the fact that living an alternative life is somehow bolder and more courageous than pursuing any traditional calling and that it should be judged accordingly.

One afternoon, I went sailing with my dad. I told him about my plans to return to China to make a film about my experiences playing hockey there, which I'd documented in *Tropic of Hockey*. As we sailed into port, he told me, "I'm really proud and happy with what you've done with your life." He could have added, "Because, really, who thought this would all pan out?" but he didn't. Still, no one had ever said anything so fine to me in my life. And, at that moment, I was proud and happy to be a writer too.

AFTERWORD

Some of you may have noticed that there's not a sniff of information included in the previous handful of pages about blogs, web prose, e-mail writing, or digi-books. This is not an accident. I've purposefully avoided exploring these subjects because of the changing nature of our times: Listservs giving way to MySpaces giving way to FaceBooks, et al. I've stuck, mostly, to the reliable mediums – books, newspapers, and magazines – which have proven to be formidable over hundreds of years while digi-forms are still relatively new and unproven. This is not to say that traditional writing won't eventually give way to a new wave of electronic writing. The industry is in flux, and the future of books is less predictable than it's ever been.

There's been a lot of debate among writers and publishers about the effect of the digital universe on greater literary society. I've put bits of my writing on my website (*www.davebidini.ca*), and while this hasn't punted my literary career into the stratosphere, it hasn't hurt it either. While blogs and personal websites provide readers with exposure to material, the information highway is nonetheless clogged with prose. It's unreasonable for a writer to think that he or she might rise above the mass simply by posting online. Still, one's work is better served on the table than off it. Launching prose into cyberspace through various websites devoted to e-publishing can be a good source of feedback and a great way to access a larger cyber literary community and increase your awareness of other writers (and vice versa). That said, a trip to your local bookstore can provide many of the same benefits. And somebody else makes the coffee.

Please write:
Dave Bidini
PO Box 616
Station C
Toronto, Ont
M6J 3R9

GLOSSARY

advance: a payment made by a publisher to a writer prior to the completion or publication of a manuscript

blind: when a writer submits an unsolicited (not asked for) story to a magazine, newspaper, or publisher

book: magazine staff refer to their publication as a book because it gets proofed as a bound edition before going off to the printer

byline: a line at the beginning of a news story, magazine article, or book giving the writer's name

critic (reviewer): a writer whose job is to report on the circumstances of a certain event or product and whether, in his or her opinion, the reader's time would be well spent attending the event or enjoying the product

editing: the process by which prose is altered so that it reads as well as possible

fanzine: a free or low-priced, photocopied, typewritten, or computer-generated magazine produced mostly by young writers who are fans of a specific topic, whether it be sports, music, film, or celebrities

feature: a longer journalistic story that probes the greater aspects of a subject drawn out by interviews and other sources and research

folded: when a publication ceases to publish, goes out of business

galley (galley proof): a proof of typeset text before it is made up into pages, usually in the form of long, single-column strips, used by the proofreader and author for proofreading. Galleys are still used at some magazines and newspapers, but book publishers tend to produce page proofs, where the manuscript is typeset in regular page format.

imprint: a line of specific titles issued by a publishing company *internship:* when a person volunteers to work for a period of time in the office of a magazine, newspaper, or publishing company

literary journal or magazine: a publication focused primarily on forms of literary and visual art not always found in mainstream magazines

manuscript: a complete unedited text

masthead: a box in a newspaper or magazine listing the names of owners and staff

novella: a work of fiction intermediate in length and complexity, between a short story and a novel

page proofs: a proof made from typeset material arranged in regular page format. After corrections have been made, a revised proof is prepared.

pitching (a proposal): the process by which a writer explains to an editor or publisher what a proposed article will be like before he or she actually writes it

press box: the section of an arena high above the rink or playing field where people who work for the media observe sports or entertainment events

press pass: a laminated card that gives the reviewer (critic) access to the press box and other comfortable sections with a good view of the arena or theater, as well as access to backstage

proofreading (proofed): the process by which printed text is read by one or more proofreaders for printing, spelling, or grammatical errors

prose: any kind of writing that's not in verse form (poetry)

publisher: the person who oversees the operation of a magazine, newspaper, or publishing company. He or she hires most of the staff, creates a vision for the publication, and raises or provides the money to get it going.

put to bed: to send a completed edition of a magazine or newspaper to the printer *representation:* when a writer is represented by an agent to negotiate his or her contracts and other publishing deals

review: a critical evaluation of an event or product (such as a play or book)

reviewer: a writer whose job is to report on the circumstances of a certain event or product and whether, in his or her opinion, the reader's time would be well spent attending the event or enjoying the product

semantics: the branch of linguistics concerned with the interpretation or meaning of words

senior editor: the person who oversees the editorial staff and sometimes but not always edits the contributing.writers' work. The senior editor is the publisher's eyes and ears within the organization.

sidebar: a short, usually boxed article in a newspaper or magazine placed alongside a main article and containing additional or explanatory material

stringer: a newspaper correspondent not on the regular staff, especially one retained on a freelance basis to report on events in a particular place

typeset/typesetting: to set original manuscripts in type to recreate a galley or page proof for proofreading

unsolicited: not asked for